Leopold Mozart's Notebook for Wolfgang Arranged for Ukulele

by Ondřej Šárek

1 2

Visit us on the Web at www.melbay.com — E-mail us at email@melbay.com

Contents

Introduction

Wolfgang Amadeus Mozart is certainly the most famous composer, and not only he, but also other members of Mozart family, were very musically gifted. Even his father, Leopold Mozart, was a famous composer.

This book connects both of these composers. When Wolfgang was seven years old, he received a notebook, "Notebook for Wolfgang," as a birthday present from his father. In this book there are contemporary dances and arias which were composed mostly by Leopold Mozart. A few songs were even added from other authors.

For this book I have chosen fifteen pieces from "Notebook for Wolfgang" and arranged them for ukulele. In these compositions we can explore Wolfgang Amadeus Mozart and how he became such a great composer.

How to Read Tablature

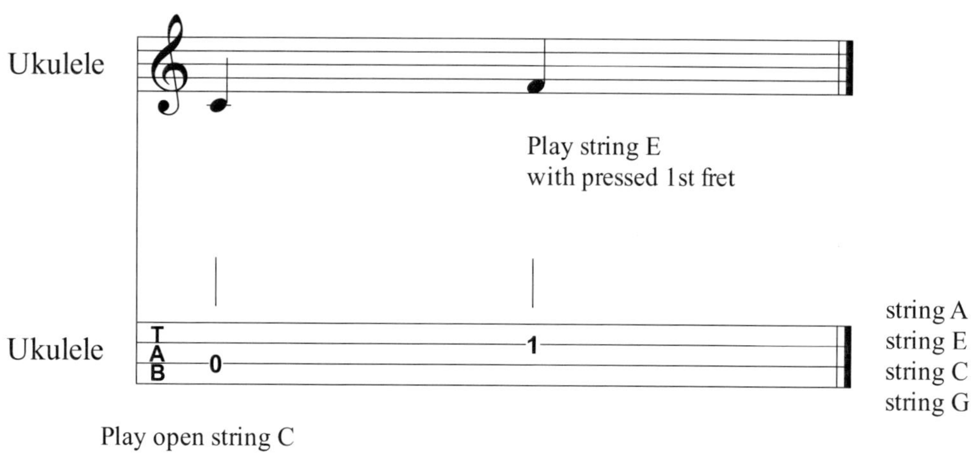

Menuet

Leopold Mozart
arr: Ondřej Šárek

Menuet

Sigr. Bach
arr: Ondřej Šárek

Bourlesq

Alte Volksweise
arr: Ondřej Šárek

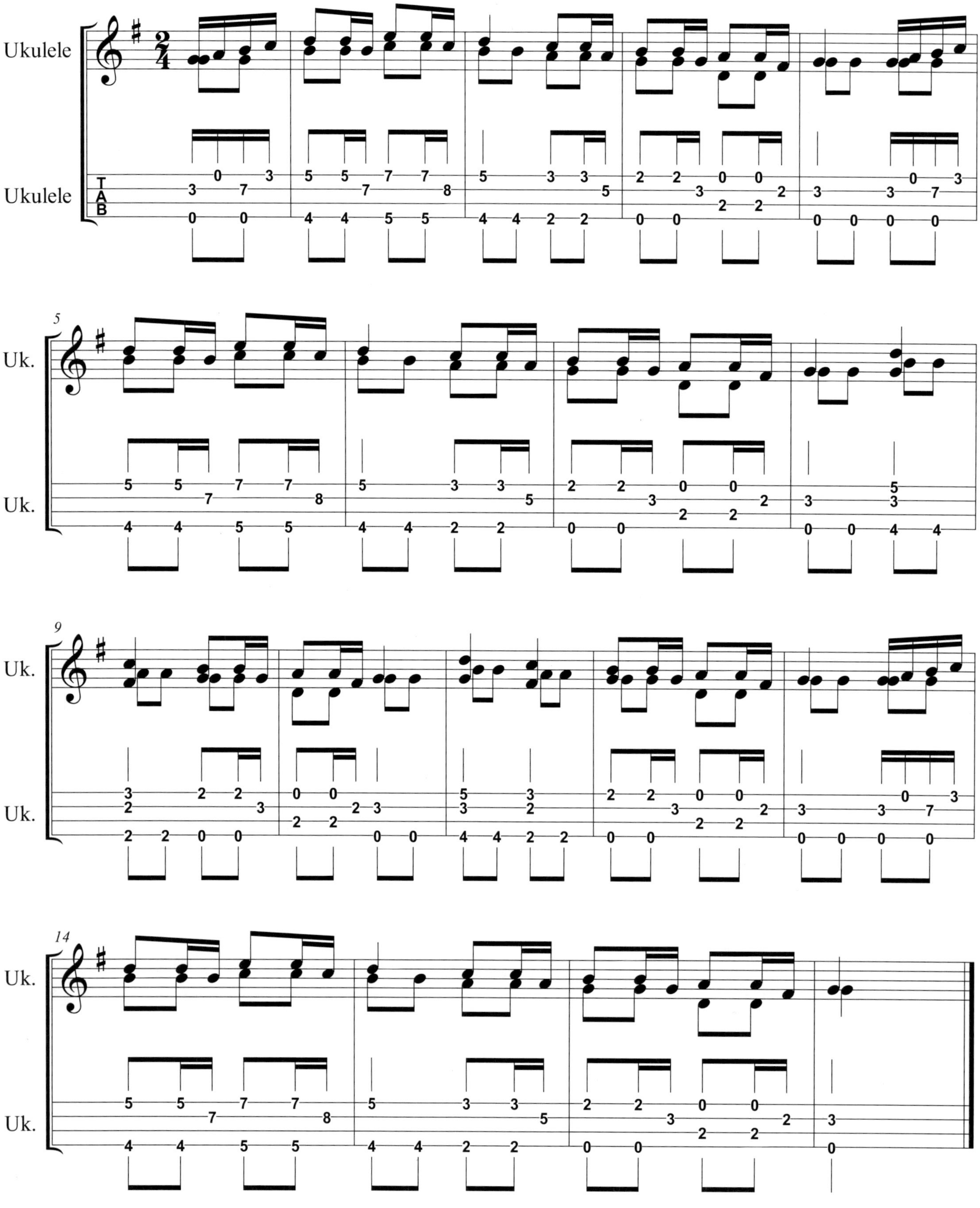

Menuet

Johann Adolph Hasse
arr: Ondřej Šárek

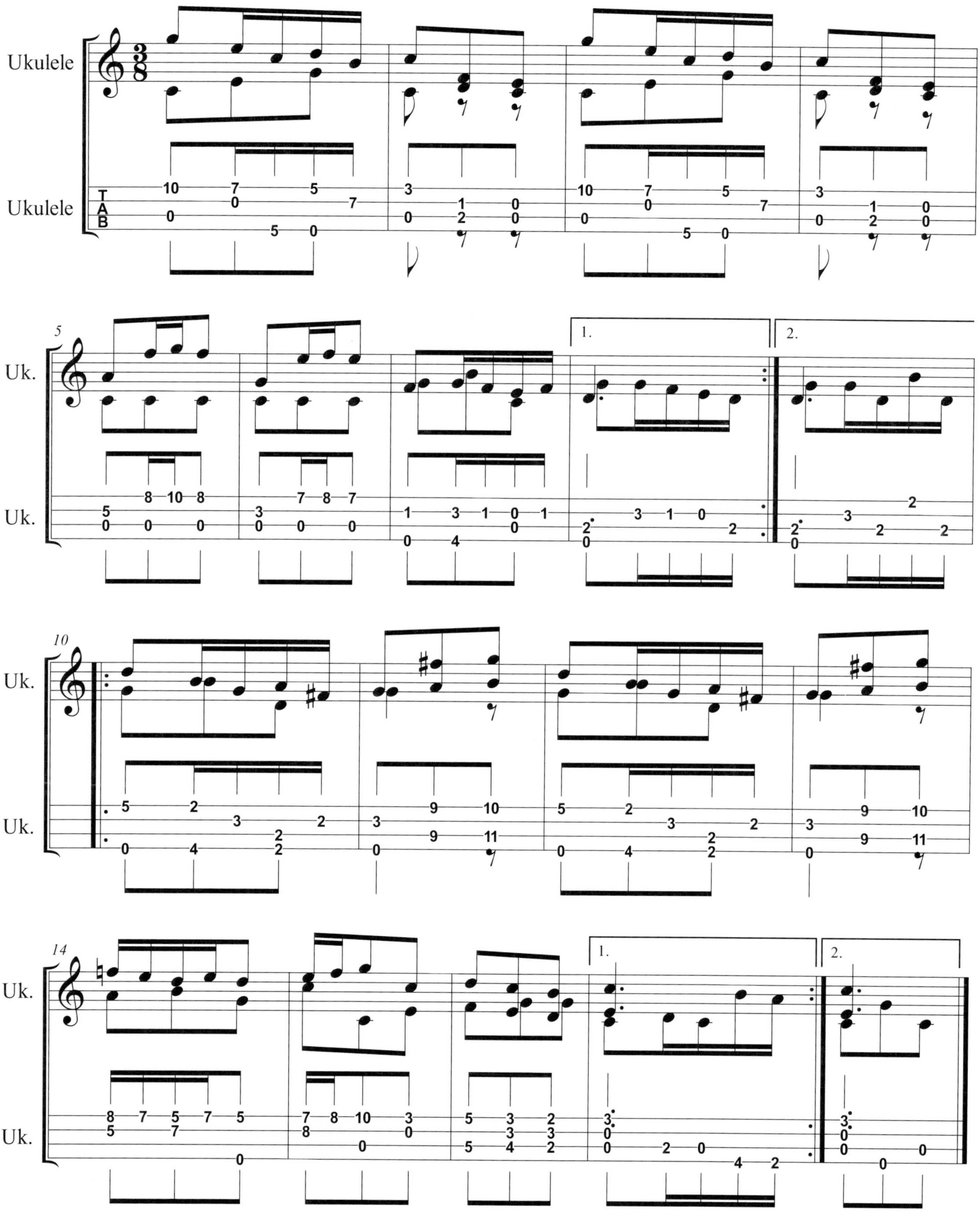

Polonaise

Johann Georg Leopold Mozart
arr: Ondřej Šárek

Entrée

Johann Georg Leopold Mozart
arr: Ondřej Šárek

Bourrée

Johann Georg Leopold Mozart
arr: Ondřej Šárek

Polonaise

Johann Georg Leopold Mozart
arr: Ondřej Šárek

Schwaben Tanz

German Dance
arr: Ondřej Šárek

14
Uk.
Uk.
17
Uk.
Uk.
20
Uk.
Uk.
23
Uk.
Uk.

Menuet

Johann Georg Leopold Mozart
arr: Ondřej Šárek

13
Uk.
Uk.
16
Uk.
Uk.
19
Uk.
Uk.
22
Uk.
Uk.

Menuet

Johann Georg Leopold Mozart
arr: Ondřej Šárek

Uk.
Uk.

Passepied

Johann Georg Leopold Mozart
arr: Ondřej Šárek

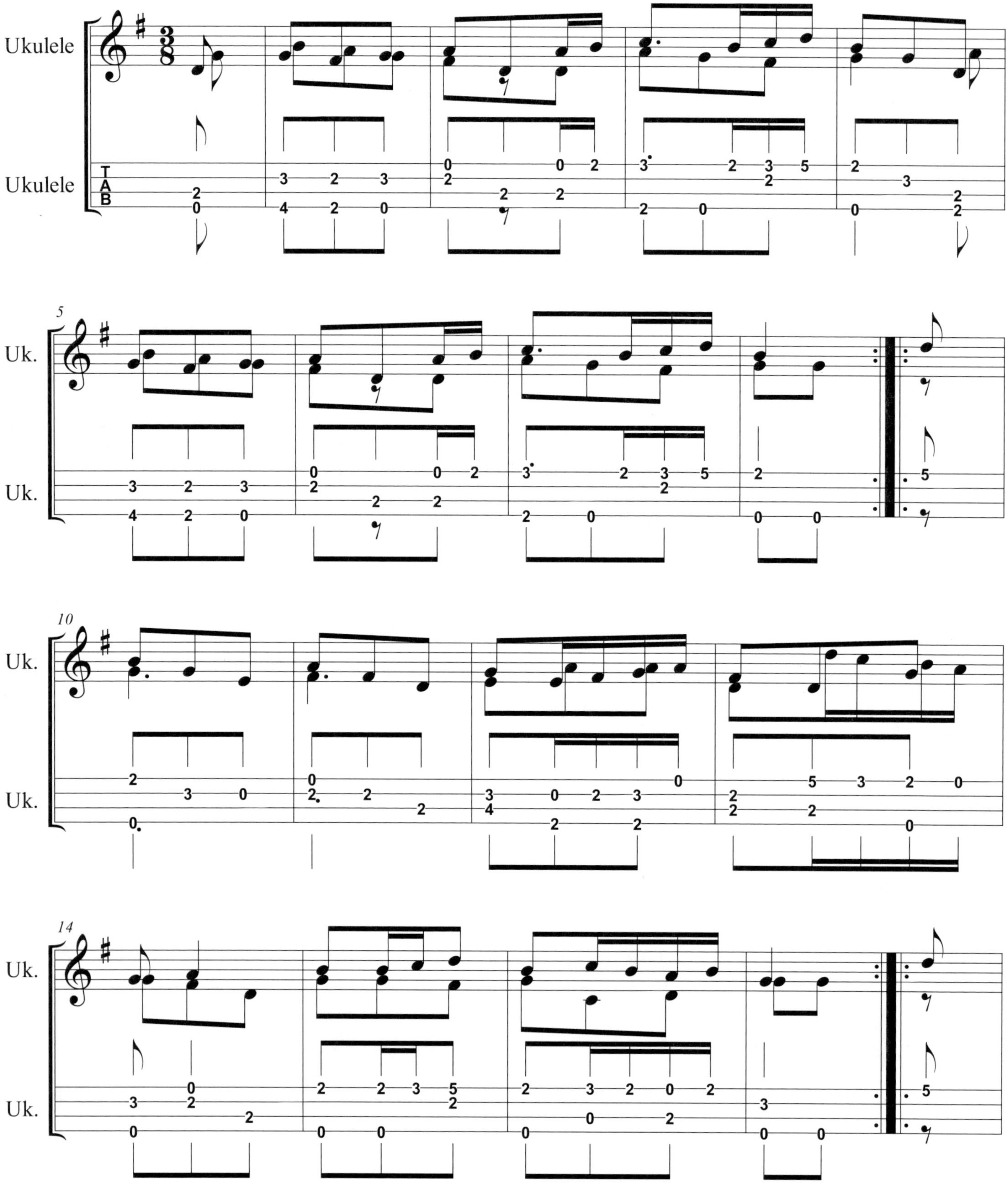

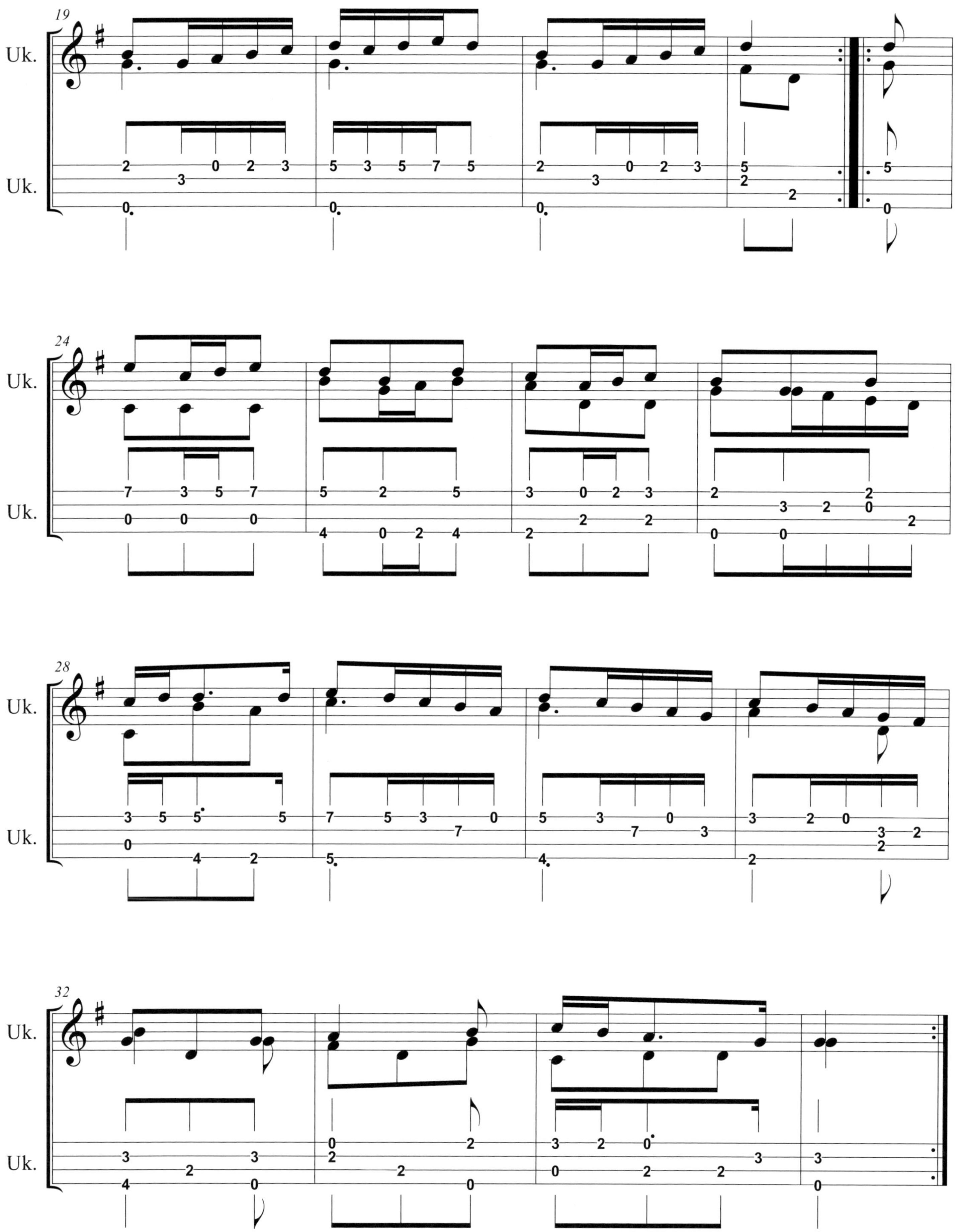
19
Uk.
Uk.
24
Uk.
Uk.
28
Uk.
Uk.
32
Uk.
Uk.

Aria

Johann Georg Leopold Mozart
arr: Ondřej Šárek

Menuet

Johann Georg Leopold Mozart
arr: Ondřej Šárek

Polonaise

Johann Georg Leopold Mozart
arr: Ondřej Šárek

MEL BAY®